Water Rides

by Grace Hansen

AMUSEMENT PARK RIDES

Abdo Kids Jumbo is an Imprint of Abdo Kids
abdopublishing.com

abdopublishing.com

Published by Abdo Kids, a division of ABDO, P.O. Box 398166, Minneapolis, Minnesota 55439.
Copyright © 2019 by Abdo Consulting Group, Inc. International copyrights reserved in all countries.
No part of this book may be reproduced in any form without written permission from the publisher.
Abdo Kids Jumbo™ is a trademark and logo of Abdo Kids.

052018

092018

THIS BOOK CONTAINS
RECYCLED MATERIALS

Photo Credits: Alamy, Getty Images, iStock, Shutterstock

Production Contributors: Teddy Borth, Jennie Forsberg, Grace Hansen

Design Contributors: Dorothy Toth, Laura Mitchell

Library of Congress Control Number: 2017960580

Publisher's Cataloging-in-Publication Data

Names: Hansen, Grace, author.

Title: Water rides / by Grace Hansen.

Description: Minneapolis, Minnesota : Abdo Kids, 2019. | Series: Amusement park rides |
    Includes glossary, index and online resources (page 24).

Identifiers: ISBN 9781532108051 (lib.bdg.) | ISBN 9781532109034 (ebook) |
    ISBN 9781532109522 (Read-to-me ebook)

Subjects: LCSH: Water--Juvenile literature. | Amusement rides--Juvenile literature. |
    Amusement parks--Juvenile literature.

Classification: DDC 791.068--dc23

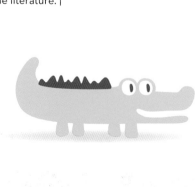

Table of Contents

The Good Old Days

Some of the first water rides were called old mills. People enjoyed them. But they did not move very fast.

4

5

The Pirates of the Caribbean ride opened in Disneyland in the 1960s. It is a river cave ride. It is based on early old mill rides.

7

A Shoot-the-Chute was built at Coney Island in 1895. A cable pulled a boat to the top of the ride. The boat slid down the ramp and into a lagoon.

In 1923, Herbert Sellner of Minnesota made one of the first water slides. It was called the Water-Toboggan Slide. Riders flew down on wooden sleds into a lake.

11

Chutes & Flumes

Shoot the chutes and **flumes** are still popular today. Splash Mountain is a Disney ride. It makes a big splash at the bottom!

Ragers & Racers

River rapids rides have smaller drops than chutes and **flumes**. But the waters are raging!

Racing slides let riders go against each other. Some are big enough for 10 racers!

The Biggest and Best

Mount Kilimanjaro is the tallest water slide in the world. It is 164 feet (50 m) tall. Riders reach speeds of 57 miles an hour (91.7 km/h)!

19

All water rides are popular.

There are entire parks devoted

to water rides! Happy Magic

Water Cube is in Beijing, China.

More Facts

- The Leap of Faith at the Atlantis in the Bahamas has a 60-foot (18.3 m) drop. Riders slide down and into a clear tunnel. The tunnel shoots through a lagoon filled with sharks!

- Mammoth Water Coaster is one of the longest water slides at 1,763 feet (537.4 m)!

- The Mount Kilimanjaro water slide is in Brazil. One out of three people decide not to go down the slide once they reach the top.

Glossary

Coney Island – in Brooklyn, New York, it was the largest amusement park area in the United States between 1880 and 1940.

flume – a deep, narrow channel with a stream running through it.

lagoon – an artificial pool or a shallow body of water that is separated from a larger body of water.

Index

Abdo Kids
ONLINE
FREE! ONLINE MULTIMEDIA RESOURCES

Visit **abdokids.com** and use this code to access crafts, games, videos, and more!

Abdo Kids Code:
AWK8051

24